Furry Logic

laugh at life

Other Books by Jane Seabrook

Furry Logic: A Guide to Life's Little Challenges

Furry Logic Parenthood

Furry Logic

laugh at life

Jane Seabrook

Andrews McMeel
Publishing

Kansas City

For Mark, Clare & Jamie

Warning: This message contains

Thought and Thought by-products.

Proceed with caution.

Would

you

like to

speak

to the

man in

charge . . .

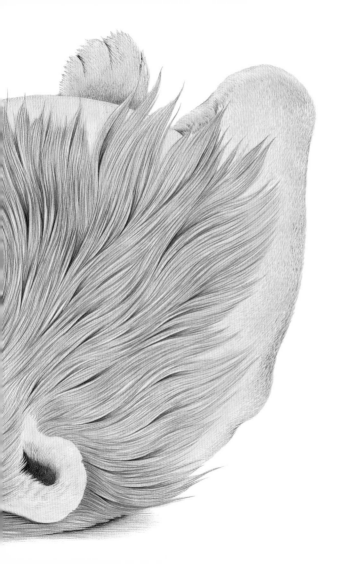

or

the

woman

who

knows

what's

happening?

There's no problem so big or complicated

that it can't be run away from.

Always take a lawyer with you.

And bring another

lawyer to watch him.

Those are my principles,

and if you don't like them . . .

well, I have others.

I always try to go

the extra mile at work,

but my boss always finds me . . .

and brings   me back.

My take-home pay

doesn't even

take me home.

Job placement: Telling your boss what he

can do with your job.

Just let me **shop** *. . .*

and no one will get hurt!

Saw it, wanted it, threw a tantrum,

Got It!

At the end of the money,

I always have some month left.

If there's no chocolate

in heaven,

I'm not going.

Every time I hear the word "exercise,"

I wash my mouth out with chocolate.

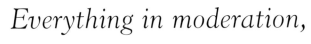

Everything in moderation,

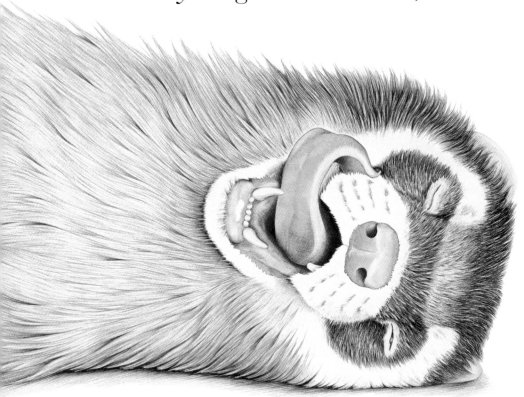

including moderation.

Lead me

not into temptation.

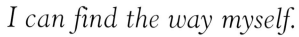

I can find the way myself.

Okay! I love you!

Now can we eat?

Princess, having had sufficient

experience with princes, seeks frog.

I love being married.

It's great to find that one special person
you want to annoy for the rest of your life.

The

moment

for calm and

rational

discussion

is past.

Now is

the time

for

senseless

bickering.

Out of estrogen.

Next mood swing:

two minutes.

Women like silent men — they think . . .

they're listening.

I hate repeating gossip — but really, what else can you do with it?

As you get older,

your secrets are safe with

your friends because they

can't remember them either.

Middle age is when we

can do just as much as ever—

but would rather not.

Don't worry

about avoiding temptation.

As you grow older,

it will avoid you.

My

wild oats

have turned into prunes and All-Bran.

Forget

health food.

I'm at an age where I need all

the preservatives I can get.

Now that food has

replaced sex in my life,

I can't even get into

my own pants.

Don't get lost in the shuffle.

Shuffle along with the lost.

I live in my own little world.

But it's okay — they know me here.

Gone crazy.

Back soon.

Artist's notes

I'm not a natural writer of one-liners, unlike the plumber who scribbled "Gone crazy back soon" on a torn piece of cardboard and left it in the window of his van. So I'm grateful to the clever people whose lines I've

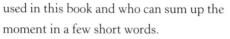

used in this book and who can sum up the moment in a few short words.

One of the most enjoyable tasks in putting together a Furry Logic book is assembling these collected thoughts into just the right order to make the book flow smoothly. The way I accomplish this is not very high tech—I lay out dozens of scraps of paper on the floor, shuffling them around until the sequence works. Once the gems of wisdom are organized into a sort of skeleton for the book, I start working on the watercolor paintings that will bring it all to life. If you would like some tips on the watercolor techniques I use, or for more information on the Furry Logic series of books, visit www.janeseabrook.com.

Keep sending me your messages via the Web site. I love to receive them, I try to write back, and it is a great inspiration when I am painting the next Furry Logic book.

Best wishes, Jane.

Acknowledgments

A special thank-you for their support and encouragement to Mark Seabrook-Davison, Diana Robinson, and Alison Davison. A big thank-you also to Alex Trimbach, Troy Caltaux, Debby Heard Photography, Joy Willis, and printers Ricky Cheng and Mr. Cheung at Phoenix Offset.

Grateful thanks to Ashleigh Brilliant for permission to print *The moment for calm and rational discussion is past. Now is the time for senseless bickering.* The words are derived from the original Pot-Shot #1019 *The time for action is past! Now is the time for senseless bickering.* Copyright 1977 by Ashleigh Brilliant, www.ashleighbrilliant.com.

Thank you to John Coney of *Grapevine* magazine in Auckland, New Zealand, for many of the quotations attributable to "Anon." Other quotations appeared or are quoted in the following publications: *Middle age is when we can do just as much as ever–but would rather not* and *There's no problem so big or complicated that it can't be run away from* in *The Penguin Dictionary of Modern Humorous Quotations*, edited by Fred Metcalf, Penguin Group, UK. *I hate repeating gossip–but really, what else can you do with it?* in *The Penguin Dictionary of Jokes*, compiled by Fred Metcalf, Penguin Group, UK.

Furry Logic Who's Who

Because I'm sometimes asked to identify the animals I've painted,
I've named most of them here, including the more obscure ones
such as the one-wattled cassowary from the jungle in New Guinea
and the secretary bird (so named for the quill-like feathers at the
back of its head) from the African plains.

1. Red-eyed tree frog 2. Chameleon 3. Hornbill

4. Prairie dog 5. Heron 6. Black grouse 7. Crowned crane

8. Rockhopper penguin 9. Meerkat 10. Chipmunk 11. Ferret

12. Siberian tiger 13.Scarlet macaw 14. Carmine bee-eater

15. Lioness 16. Amazon parrot 17. Blue and yellow macaw

18. Sea lion 19. Great horned owl 20. Prairie dog

21. One-wattled cassowary 22. Camel 23. Secretary bird

24. King penguin 25. Tarsier 26. Grizzly bear

For more information visit www.janeseabrook.com.